How to Be *Free* from
DEPRESSION

Biblical Hope and Help for
Dealing with Depression,
Guilt, and Self-Esteem

JIM WILSON

COMMUNITY CHRISTIAN MINISTRIES
MOSCOW, IDAHO

Published by Community Christian Ministries
P.O. Box 9754, Moscow, Idaho 83843
208.883.0997 | www.ccmbooks.org

Jim Wilson, *How to Be Free from Depression*
Reprinted from *How to Be Free*
Copyright © 2022 by Community Christian Ministries.

Cover by Samuel Dickison.
Interior design by Valerie Anne Bost.

Printed in the United States of America.

All rights reserved. No part of this publication may be reproduced, stored in a retrieval system, or transmitted in any form by any means, electronic, mechanical, photocopy, recording, or otherwise, without prior permission of the copyright holder, except as provided by USA copyright law.

Unless otherwise stated, all Scripture quotations are from the the Holy Bible, New International Version®, NIV® Copyright © 1973, 1978, 1984, 2011 by Biblica, Inc.® Used by permission. All rights reserved worldwide.

Scripture quotations marked KJV are from the King James Version, which is in the public domain.

Scripture quotations marked NKJV are from the New King James Version®, copyright © 1982 by Thomas Nelson. Used by permission. All rights reserved.

CONTENTS

Introduction 1

1   How to Be Free from Depression 5

2   How to Be Free from False Guilt 17

3   How to Be Free from Low Self-Esteem 29

4   How to Walk in the Light 37

INTRODUCTION

IT IS COMMON FOR CHRISTIANS to believe that we are each enslaved to particular sins. The truth is that we are not slaves. If you are a Christian, *you are already free.*

> Since the children have flesh and blood, he too shared in their humanity so that by his death he might break the power of him who holds the power of death—that is, the devil—and *free* those who all their lives were held in slavery by their fear of death. (Heb. 2:14–15)

> It is for freedom that Christ has set us free. Stand firm, then, and do not let yourselves be burdened again by a yoke of slavery. (Gal. 5:1)

So if the Son sets you free, you will be free indeed. (John 8:36)

We are free indeed. What are we to do with this freedom? "Be ye therefore perfect, *even as your Father which is in heaven is perfect*" (Matt. 5:48, KJV). How can we do that? This verse tells us how—imitate God.

"But love your enemies, do good to them, and lend to them without expecting to get anything back. Then your reward will be great, and you will be sons of the Most High, because he is kind to the ungrateful and wicked. Be merciful, *just as your Father is merciful*" (Luke 6:35–36). Jesus told us to love our enemies. How? Imitate God by being merciful.

> Get rid of all bitterness, rage and anger, brawling and slander, along with every form of malice. Be kind and compassionate to one another, forgiving each other, just as in Christ God forgave you. Be imitators of God, therefore, as dearly loved children. (Eph. 4:31–5:1)

If unsaved people were commanded to imitate God, that command would make no sense. They are captive to Satan and unable to imitate God. "Those who oppose him he must gently instruct, in the hope that God will grant them repentance leading them to a knowledge of the truth, and that they will come to their senses and

INTRODUCTION

escape from the trap of the devil, who has taken them captive to do his will" (2 Tim. 2:25–26).

"And you will know the truth, and the truth will make you free" (John 8:32). We are free, and because of that we have the ability to imitate God.

> . . . because through Christ Jesus the law of the Spirit who gives life has set me free from the law of sin and death. (Rom. 8:2)

Chapter 1
HOW TO BE FREE FROM DEPRESSION

THERE ARE THREE KINDS OF depression: biological, psychological, and spiritual. Depression is not necessarily just a spiritual problem. However, even a biological phenomenon can turn into a spiritual problem. How you feel physically can be a *temptation* to spiritual depression. If you suddenly contract a disease that renders you lethargic or incapacitated, especially for a long period of time, it can make you depressed.

If you anticipate those feelings, the biological causes can be addressed before they lead to depression. Consider the biological cause as a *temptation* to sinful depression. What caused you to feel low may be physical, but if you get down and stay down, that is sin. There is a command against it: "Rejoice in the Lord always" (Phil. 4:4). Your depression may not be caused by sin (e.g., you might be depressed because you have cancer and are constantly ill and fatigued, not because you have violated one of the Ten Commandments), but the depression itself is still sin.

Another biological temptation happens to women regularly. At a certain time of the month, a woman's menstrual cycle results in a great hormonal temptation to irritability. I learned this fact the slow way. After Bessie and I were married, I began to realize that something made her act erratically at certain times, and it seemed to be periodic. Being a dumb young husband, I was puzzled for a while. Finally, I figured out what it was.

I questioned Bessie about it. "Tell me, is this event predictable?" She said yes. "Then I would like you to let me know several days ahead of time, and I will walk softly. I will be kinder and more considerate than is normally necessary, and I will pray with you that this will not be a temptation that ends in sin." We did that for many years with great success.

Some depression is psychological. Psychological depression is largely based upon relational situations—peer pressure, family pressure, anxiety, etc. These stresses are temptations to depression, but not excuses for it.

Recognizing them for what they are at the outset is a good way to prevent them from turning into depression.

Once you are depressed, you can be easily swamped by the feelings that come with depression: "I'm no good, I'm worthless, God can't or won't forgive me, everybody hates me, and they should." Regardless of how it started, when you get into this situation, you are in sin. This is a difficult thing to tell a depressed person, because it is what he wants to hear. "Yeah, you're right. I'm in sin." It feeds his depression. But it is not the kind of sin that he or she thinks it is. The sin of "I think I'll go eat worms" depression is *believing something about the character of God that is not true.* It is the sin of believing lies from the devil about God, about yourself, about everyone. "God can't and won't forgive me" is a *lie*.

If a person is only a little depressed, he can understand this fairly easily. But sometimes we can be so completely lost in depression that whatever someone else says makes no sense. They could say funny things, true things, false things, and we just do not hear them.

One time, a woman came to my noon Bible study at Washington State University. I could see she was not getting much out of the first hour. In the interval before the second hour, she hung around. She was a Christian, and she had come to the study hoping to talk to me. I approached her to say something (I do not remember what), and she just broke down in tears. I had to send the rest of the class home.

I spent an hour with her. I tried to make sense. She was not getting it. I tried to explain, but it did not sink in. I decided to try getting through to her by repetition. So for most of the hour I repeated this one sentence over and over again: *Go home and tell the devil he's a liar.* I yelled and hollered and just kept repeating *Go home and tell the devil he's a liar!* Finally, it got through.

What is depression? *Depression is believing a lie of the devil and not believing the character and the truth of God.* This woman had been in awful depression for months. At church the following Sunday, she gave one of the greatest testimonies I have ever heard. She had gone home and told the devil that he was a liar and that she was not going to believe him anymore. What I told her made a great difference. Depression springs from believing things that are coming straight from the devil.

When you are depressed, write down every thought you have, whether they are thoughts about yourself, God, or other people. After you have them all written down, get a concordance and look up references for each of these thoughts that supposedly come from God. You will not find any of them in Scripture. All of them are clearly from the enemy. They are lies. That is why depression is connected with sin, even if it has a biological or psychological source: once you are depressed, you start believing things that are not true.

Another problem with depression is that when a depressed person reads the Scripture, he does not find all the wonderful verses; he finds every one that mentions sinning and going to hell. Instead, look up all the positive promises of God. Write them out for yourself. Paste them on your refrigerator or on your bathroom mirror. Recite them out loud to yourself throughout the day. Saturate yourself in the truth of God's loving thoughts toward you. (If you know someone who is very depressed, you may have to help him do each of these things.)

Sometimes you just have to buckle down and fight your way out of the depression. You may not feel like doing the things that will pull you out, but make yourself do them anyway. Use any method to keep yourself from giving in and agreeing with the thoughts that are going through your head. Use any action to counter those lies from the devil, whether it be willpower, whether it be fighting it out yourself, whether it be calling upon God and believing. *Do not agree with the thoughts you have when you are depressed*, no matter how rational they seem or how convinced you are that they are true. *They are not true.* When you are down, of course you will not be convinced that *this* is true. I have only been depressed a few times in my life, but I remember how hard it is. When you are depressed, you do not want to believe the good things God has for you.

It is amazing that we believe things which are very clearly false and seem to be unable to believe what we know to be true. The reason for this is that this is a spiritual battle, not a rational one. Prayer in the Holy Spirit is the way to break through depression.

The Psalms are a good place to learn more about this. There are imprecatory psalms, joyful psalms, and depressed psalms. Psalms 42 and 43 are two of the depressed Psalms. The Psalmist is down in the dumps, but he shows no desire to stay that way. This is the opposite of "Nobody loves me, everybody hates me, I think I'll go eat worms" depression. The author of Psalm 42 has a great hunger to get out of it:

> As the deer pants for streams of water,
>   so my soul pants for you, O God.
> My soul thirsts for God, for the living God.
>   When can I go and meet with God?
> My tears have been my food
>   day and night,
> while men say to me all day long,
>   "Where is your God?"
> These things I remember
>   as I pour out my soul:
> how I used to go with the multitude,
>   leading the procession to the house of God,
> with shouts of joy and thanksgiving
>   among the festive throng.

Why are you downcast, O my soul?
> Why so disturbed within me?
Put your hope in God,
> *for I will yet praise him,*
> *my Savior and my God.*

My soul is downcast within me;
> therefore I will remember you
from the land of the Jordan,
> the heights of Hermon—from Mount Mizar.
Deep calls to deep
> in the roar of your waterfalls;
> all your waves and breakers
have swept over me.

By day the LORD directs his love,
> at night his song is with me—
> a prayer to the God of my life. (Ps. 42:1–8)

The Psalmist sees three things that will help him out of his depression. The first is his longing for the Lord: "My soul thirsts for God, for the living God."

The second is remembering the time when he was joyful: "These things I remember as I pour out my soul, how I used to go with the multitude, leading the procession to the house of God." He cannot comprehend singing now, but he remembers when he did sing.

Remember when you were in victory and look to the future. "For I will *yet* praise him, *my Savior and my God.*" The Psalmist is down now, but he knows that he will praise God in the future.

This is his third help. He has hope in God. *Hope* is the main way out of depression. Emily Dickinson wrote,

> "Hope" is the thing with feathers—
> That perches in the soul—
> And sings the tune without the words—
> And never stops—at all—

If you are depressed, long for God, remember what He has done for you in the past, and in faith anticipate that again in the future. This is the pattern of the rest of Psalm 42.

> I say to God my Rock,
>   "Why have you forgotten me?
> Why must I go about mourning,
>   oppressed by the enemy?"
> My bones suffer mortal agony
>   as my foes taunt me,
> saying to me all day long,
>   "Where is your God?"
>
> Why are you downcast, O my soul?
>   Why so disturbed within me?

Put your hope in God,
 for I will yet praise him,
 my Savior and my God. (Ps. 42:9–11)

The psalmist knows that God is present, but he does not feel Him there. In times like this, it is tempting to believe the devil's lie that God isn't there. It is a conflict between what the psalmist *knows* to be true and what he *feels* at the moment. The subjective "truth" says, "Why have you forgotten me?" But he has the objective truth that God is his rock, and it is that truth that will pull him up.

There are different reasons for the depression that is recorded in the Psalms, but within each Psalm there is always an answer to that depression. If anyone says to you, "God has forsaken me. He must have left me, because I don't feel Him," he is saying the same thing as Psalm 42. But firm hope in a sure thing will get him out of depression. When David got depressed, he preached to himself: "Put your hope in God, for I will yet praise him, my Savior and my God." If you are depressed, keep pointing yourself back to *the love of God for you*, regardless of how you feel. Try to create a thirst, a longing for God. Stir yourself up to remember the time when you did rejoice in the Lord and remind yourself that you are going to rejoice again.

Read through the Scriptures and search for all the verses on God's love and kindness. When you find one, ask yourself if it is true or false. Read the verse out loud to yourself and make yourself answer *true* out loud. Thank God out loud that it is true. That will help you get it into your heart. Here is one to get you started: "*For the Father Himself loves you*, because you have loved Me, and have believed that I came forth from God" (John 16:27, NKJV).

One thing that often accompanies (and occasionally causes) depression is guilt. Some secular psychologists teach that guilt is wrong because it brings you down, so you should not feel guilty. Of course, because a person who is guilty is not rejoicing in the Lord, he does need to get rid of the guilt. Because they do not have a real solution for real guilt, non-Christians will teach that the guilt *itself* is wrong, rather than acknowledging that the guilt is a *thermometer* of wrong. They teach you to accept your lying as normal, to accept your adultery as all right, so that you do not feel guilty, because the guilt is killing you. The secular psychologist's solution is to accept yourself as you are, to say that evil is good.

You *do* need to get rid of the guilt, but that is the wrong way to do it. Scripture says no to it. Real guilt is caused by a violation of the holiness of God. Only the death and resurrection of Jesus Christ can take care of that guilt when we believe in Him and confess our sin.

"Godly sorrow brings repentance that leads to salvation and leaves no regret, but worldly sorrow brings death" (2 Cor. 7:10). Godly sorrow causes repentance; the sorrow of this world causes death. But sorrow and guilt are often related. We can be sorry about something that is wrong and not repent of it, feeling that there is some sort of virtue in feeling sorry. We think that if we feel guilty long enough, we will have paid for our sin. This is using penance in place of repentance, and it is wrong. Godly sorrow causes *repentance*, and when repentance takes place, the sorrow and the guilt are taken away.

When you are dealing with guilt or depression, remember the greatness of God and His constancy and steadfastness. In my unconverted days, I was depressed much of the time. I was converted under the preaching of Psalm 40: "I waited patiently for the Lord; he turned to me and heard my cry. He lifted me out of the slimy pit, out of the mud and mire; he set my feet on a rock and gave me a firm place to stand" (vv. 1–2).

Depression is a slimy, miry pit. This is my salvation: "He put a new song in my mouth, a hymn of praise to our God" (Ps. 40:3a).

Chapter 2

HOW TO BE FREE FROM FALSE GUILT

REAL GUILT IS TAKEN CARE OF in the cross. There is one condition for the Christian to be forgiven, and that is that he admits his sin before a holy God.

False guilt does not come from God. It is laid on us by the enemy. It concerns things that are not wrong, but that the enemy tells us *are* wrong. When we confess them to God, God doesn't forgive them, because they're not sin. The enemy doesn't forgive them, because he doesn't forgive anything. So we walk around with a continual shadow of guilt.

False guilt comes from holding yourself to man's standards instead of to God's. It is a corollary to legalism.

Most people have experienced false guilt at some point. The ones who give it to you the most are those closest to you—yourself, your parents, your husband, wife, roommate, boyfriend, or girlfriend—because you pay attention to their standards.

What is the difference? If you bend the rules at work (for example, rationalizing that because you are a good worker it is OK to take an extra hour off), that is wrong unless you have permission from the boss, and what you end up feeling is real guilt. False guilt occurs when you set higher standards for yourself than the Bible does. Suppose you decide that something has to be done by the first of the month. This is not something your boss has determined; you just set the deadline for yourself. For whatever reason, you do not get to it until the second of the month. You feel guilty because you violated your own stupid rule. It was not a moral rule; it was not God's rule. It was man's rule (and not even some other man's, but your own). Perfectionists do this all the time. They set up false standards, fail to meet them, and feel guilty. This is false guilt.

Some people even feel guilty for others who are not meeting the standards they have set themselves. They feel guilty for *you*, even though your "failure" has nothing to do with them. For example, an acquaintance of mine had a habit of writing in his Bible. One of his friends could not see how writing in God's Holy Word was right and told him he should be ashamed of himself. He did not intend to condemn his friend at all; he simply felt awful for him because he was writing in the margins in his Bible.

Churches can also impose extrabiblical rules on their congregations. This kind of legalism is not such an open-and-shut issue. The Bible speaks of *voluntary* abstinence from certain things (e.g., eating meat, drinking alcohol). If you want to follow these kinds of rules, that is fine, but you should *not* feel guilty if you do not follow them. That is the difference between deciding to follow a set of extrabiblical rules yourself and trying to impose those same rules on others. As Christians, we are allowed to follow any extra set of rules we want to as long as they do not violate Scripture, but we should not feel guilty for failing to follow them since they are not rules that *God* set for us.

Perfectionists' biggest problem is often with people who are not as strict about time, order, and cleanliness as they are. These things are so important to the perfectionist that he has a hard time comprehending that the person who "fails" in them is not in sin. He can describe their failure so that it begins to look immoral: extenuating circumstances that will result from you not cleaning your room, ramifications to the witness of the church, etc. He can make it sound like a terribly serious matter that you did not comb your hair this morning.

Conversely, Christians who are not perfectionists need to be careful not to stumble their perfectionist brothers. Leaving the newspaper on the floor is not immoral. But suppose leaving your newspaper on the floor frustrates your roommate, who thinks it *is* immoral. In that case, you probably ought to pick up the paper for the sake of his conscience. He is the weaker brother from Romans 14:

> Accept him whose faith is weak, without passing judgment on disputable matters. One man's faith allows him to eat everything, but another man, whose faith is weak, eats only vegetables. The man who eats everything must not look down on him who does not, and the man who does not eat everything must not condemn the man who does, for God has accepted him. Who are you to judge someone else's servant? To his own master he stands or falls. And he will stand, for the Lord is able to make him stand....
>
> Therefore let us stop passing judgment on one another. Instead, make up your mind not to put any stumbling block or obstacle in your brother's way. As one who is in the Lord Jesus, I am fully convinced that no food is unclean in itself. But if anyone regards something as unclean, then for him it is unclean. If your brother is distressed because of what you eat, you are no longer acting in love. Do not by your eating destroy your brother for whom Christ died. (Rom. 14:1–4, 13–15)

Sin is violating the Word of God. If for the purposes of your own discipline you wish to have additional standards above and beyond or different from that (but not contrary to it), do not call it sin when you do not keep them, and do not call it sin when someone else does not keep them. The Bible condemns enough sins without us adding to them. These other things will not get forgiven. They *cannot* be forgiven, because they are not sin.

Suppose you have an appointment to meet someone at a certain time, and you are held up by an event beyond your control: a freight train went off the rail and blocked the road, or you had an opportunity to talk to someone and you could not get out of it. You wind up being twenty minutes late. In a case like this, you are not guilty in God's eyes. You were in the will of God waiting for the freight train, or you were in the will of God talking to that person. There is no sin, and therefore there should be no guilt. But you arrived twenty minutes late, and the person who was waiting for you looks at you in an accusing fashion, and you feel guilty. In fact, you probably felt guilty even before you got there, so you already started figuring out an explanation. Even after you explain, you still feel guilty because people generally do not forgive, even though they may acknowledge your explanation. However, your delay was not wrong in the first place.

Imagine now that you did two things in the course of a week. First, you told a big, fat lie. Second, you missed the morning session at a Christian conference by being somewhere else you needed to be. You show up at the conference the next day, and the saints say, "Where were you yesterday?" Let's assume for the sake of argument that you were in the will of God by not being at that conference. You were somewhere God wanted you. When everyone looks at you and says, "Where were you?" you feel guilty. Here you have two guilts: one, a real sin against a real, holy God, and the other not sin at all. You feel the same guilt for lying as for missing the conference, so you confess both.

God does not have a high view of liars. He tells us that He has prepared a lake of fire for them. But when you confess this lie to the Lord God, He forgives it, and it's gone.

Then you confess missing the conference session, and you still feel guilty. Why? First off, God does not forgive things that are *not sin*. Second, what made you feel guilty was people, and people very often don't forgive. They hold it over you so that you won't do it again. One of the ways you can learn to recognize false guilt is the *lack of forgiveness when you confess it*, when at the same time you have been truly forgiven for other things you did that were morally wrong.

There is another kind of false guilt. That is that when you confessed a real sin to God, God forgave it, and you don't believe it. If you are in this situation, you may not realize that what you are left with is false guilt; you may think it's something else. "It's real guilt, but I wasn't sorry enough," or, "There is some restitution that needs to be done." OK, so check those things out. If it is real guilt, confess it. If there is restitution to be made, take care of it.

If those are not the issues, assume that it's false guilt, no matter how bad you feel about it. Then look in the Scriptures to see if there is anything against this particular thing. In most cases, you won't find it. "There's something against lying." Yes, but you already confessed the lie, and God promised He would forgive you.

When you come to the conclusion (mentally, not spiritually, because you still feel guilty) that you have taken care of it every possible way that you ought to have if it were real guilt, and the guilty feeling is still there, assume that it is from the enemy, and it is false guilt.

How do you get rid of false guilt, then? Confess to God that you feel guilty for being in His will. Confess to *feeling guilty*, because that guilt has taken away your joy, and, in that sense, the false guilt itself is sin. Feeling guilty about false guilt is believing the devil. Believing the devil is sin. Confess *that*. Call *feeling guilty* a sin. "God, I've been believing the devil. He told me this is wrong. He told me You won't forgive it. Please forgive me for believing the enemy."

People who tend toward depression are very likely to be afflicted with false guilt because they pay too much attention to the opinions of men. This guilt that they cannot get rid of leads them into further depression. From there, they can get into false guilt that is very bad, even to the point of thinking their sin is unforgiveable. These Christians are in absolute despair because of what they think they are guilty of. However, they are dead wrong. They are believing the lie of the devil; they feel guilty about forgivable sin that they think is unforgivable.

So they live in *real* guilt, but not the kind of guilt they think. Usually they have a stack of real sins that have been confessed and forgiven by the Lord, but they will not accept the forgiveness. Have you ever heard anyone say, "I can't forgive myself"? That is not the problem. "Can't" means it is impossible. When someone says, "I can't," whatever the sin is, I graciously say, "No, let's say you *won't*. You won't forgive yourself." That is where the real guilt comes in.

Saying you cannot forgive yourself is a euphemism for saying that you are not responsible. You have decided not to forgive yourself because you have a higher standard of sin than God does, and you think your standard is more just. God says you are forgiven, but you say, "Sorry, God, Your standards are not high enough." Make yourself say you *will not*. This thinking is sin in itself and must be repented of.

There are also people who only believe in forgiving themselves after a period of penance—not penance in the

Roman Catholic sense, but just feeling miserable about their sin. They do not think it is legitimate to confess and be joyful again right away. But that is the only biblical way, for God tells us to "rejoice always" (Phil. 4:4).

If you are having trouble forgiving yourself, ask yourself if you would forgive someone else who had done the same sin to you. (You might want to say no, but you know that the right answer is yes.) Well then, what is the difference between you and the other person? If you would forgive the one, why will you not forgive the other?

People in this situation refuse to forgive themselves because they are consumed with how awful their sin was. We need to understand that *refusing to forgive is sin*. It is a greater sin than the one committed originally, because the Scripture says that if we will not forgive, we will not be forgiven. You need to forgive yourself. This does *not* mean saying what you did was right. Forgiveness does not say it was right. Forgiveness says it was wrong, but you are forgiven. *You do not have to think that what you did was OK.* You still have the same view of how wrong it was.

Look at Psalm 51:

> Have mercy on me, O God,
>   according to your unfailing love;
> according to your great compassion
>   blot out my transgressions.

> Wash away all my iniquity
>   and cleanse me from my sin.
> For I know my transgressions,
>   and my sin is always before me.
> Against you, you only, have I sinned
>   and done what is evil in your sight,
> so that you are proved right when you speak
>   and justified when you judge. (vv. 1–4)

There are two ways to avoid confessing sin. One is by reducing the enormity of the transgression. We want to be forgiven, but we would prefer to be forgiven for something that is not so bad. The other way to avoid confessing is to say that the sin is so bad that we or God or other people cannot forgive it. We either try to make the sin small enough that it is very easily forgivable or so big that it cannot be forgiven.

If the sin is great, it is tempting to think that there is not enough grace for it. But David had a great view of sin *and* a great view of forgiveness: "Against you, you only, have I sinned and done what is evil in your sight, so that you are proved right when you speak and justified when you judge." Whatever you do to me, God, I deserve it.

But David also says, "Have mercy on me, O God, according to your unfailing love; according to your great compassion blot out my transgressions." David had a very big view of sin and a very big view of God's abundant mercy. He knew that God's mercy was more than enough to cover his sin.

If you have sin that you think is too big, do not minimize the sin. Instead, realize that in relationship to the amount of grace God has made available for us, all it is is sin. Suppose you have committed murder. How are you ever going to get forgiven for that? Simple. It is sin, and God forgives sin. God is a great God, and His grace is *great* grace. Where sin abounds, grace abounds much more. However great your problem is, God is much, much, greater. When a person says, "God forgives me, but I can't forgive myself," he is really saying that he thinks God did not forgive him. He does not want to say that, because it is accusing God of not keeping His promise, but that is what he believes. When we really believe that God forgives us, it will not be that difficult for us to accept the forgiveness.

Sometimes you just have to call the devil a liar.

Chapter 3

HOW TO BE FREE FROM LOW SELF-ESTEEM

LOW SELF-ESTEEM IS A COMmonly diagnosed problem today. People are told that they do not love themselves enough or that they have an inferiority complex. What I have to say on this issue may sound a little harsh, but it is biblical.

The Scripture says, "Love your neighbor as yourself" (Matt. 22:39). When Jesus quoted this from the Old Testament, He was not commanding us to love ourselves. Self-love is assumed. Jesus' command was to love our neighbor. "I can't love my neighbor until I love myself," you say. That is true—but the man who thinks he does not love himself is deceiving himself. Jesus assumed that *all people love themselves*. The Bible says, "Husbands, love your wives . . . . After all, no one ever hated his own body, but he feeds and cares for it" (Eph. 5:25, 29).

Picture someone with a characteristic inferiority complex. Now answer me this: whom does that person think about most of the time? *Himself*. What he thinks about is where his love is. The person with an inferiority complex loves himself not too little, but *too much*. If he thought about his neighbor as much as he thinks about himself on a day-to-day basis, that neighbor would be loved to death. His "lack" of self-love is really inordinate self-love.

Suppose you are at a picnic and someone says, "Let's play softball." Why does that guy want to play softball? Because he plays it well. He hits a long ball; he is a good man on the bases. He wants the fun of hitting the ball, and he also does not mind everyone else knowing he can hit it. Then someone else says, "Let's not play softball; let's play horseshoes." Why does he not want to play softball? Because he strikes out, and he does not want everyone else to know it.

The first guy seems to have an extroverted personality or a superiority complex because he plays well. We assume that he has a good view of himself and that the second fellow has a poor view of himself. Hold on a moment. Whom are they both thinking about? The one wants everybody to know how far *he* hits the ball, and the other does not want anybody to know that *he* cannot hit the ball. He may have a poor view of himself when it comes to softball, but he has a good view of himself in that he does not want others to know he is bad at the game. Both people are protecting themselves. Both are thinking of themselves.

Suppose someone is always saying, "I can't do this," and, "I can't do that," and, "How awful I am . . . " He is beating himself up, but his love is still for himself. What he needs to do is get *God's* view of himself. I am not saying he does not have a problem; he *does*. It is just not the problem he thinks he has.

The solution to this is to start thinking about other people, even if you have to do it by deliberate determination. Every time you think of yourself, stop and think of so-and-so, with just as nice thoughts as you would like to think of yourself. The way you think of yourself right now might be derogatory. Aim for a *positive* thinking about someone else instead of *negative* thinking about yourself.

Get your focus off yourself and onto someone else. Suppose you find yourself in a place where you are afraid, e.g., you are sitting in the back seat of a car that someone else is driving along a mountain road, and you're thinking, "This maniac doesn't know how to drive." You wish you were out of the car. What do you do? Start interceding for other people. This applies to everything, not just to fear. Instead of praying for yourself, start praying for *other people*. It gets your mind off your own problems.

This works very well, but the only way to do it is by *choosing* to do it. It will not happen naturally. In fact, it may be very hard to do at first. Stick with it. The more you do it, the easier it will get, because your focus will be more and more on other people.

Intercession for others is not limited to praying; it is any kind of action that you give toward someone else. The best thing to do when you are stuck thinking about yourself is to think of someone who is in worse shape than you. Say, "I think I'll go call on Joe. He's really hurting." I know that in order to help Joe, I need to get grace from God. I get grace from God so that I can help Joe, and at the same time I get grace from God for me.

Other people's problems are one of the primary things that have kept me in good spiritual shape. One night when my youngest son was going to bed, he said, "I think I want to be depressed." He wanted to enjoy the misery. Often when I am out of the joy of the Lord, I will feel like staying there. Frequently, what keeps me from getting this way is other people knocking at my door with their own problems. I know I cannot share my misery with them, so I need to get grace from God for them. When I get grace for them, I get it for myself, too.

Remember that the initial problem was not that we do not love ourselves, but that we do. And we love ourselves too much in a selfish way. We have too much love, and we are not sharing it. Start sharing.

Next, get God's view of you. Read the Scriptures, and you will find out that God's love for you is not love *because*. Suppose you "don't love yourself" because you have a particular habit you can't shake. Remember that word *can't* from the last chapter. It is wrong. You have a habit that you *won't* shake, so you sit around thinking negative thoughts about yourself. God's view of man is very realistic. He says we are bad news. But He also says, "I love you, and I have many good thoughts toward you." God does not say, "You are good; therefore, I have good thoughts toward you." He says, "You are *bad*; therefore, I have *good* thoughts."

"Many, O Lord my God, are thy wonderful works which thou hast done, and thy thoughts which are to us-ward: they cannot be reckoned up in order unto thee: if I would declare and speak of them, they are more than can be numbered" (Psalm 40:5, KJV). If I tried to speak of all the wondrous deeds that God has done for me and all the wondrous thoughts He has toward me, I could not do it. There are too many. God thinks good things toward me. When I begin to think about myself the way He does, that is a healthy view. Then I find it easier to teach and preach.

Romans 12:3 says, "Do not think of yourself more highly than you ought." It does not say, "more lowly than you ought." The reason it does not say that is that thinking too lowly of ourselves is not our problem. God assumes that we love ourselves, but He does not assume it is healthy when it stops at that. That is a selfish love. That is not God's kind of love toward us. Paul says that if we have God's view of His love toward us, and we go and love others in the same way that we have loved ourselves and that God loves us, we have fulfilled the law.

> A new command I give you: Love one another. As I have loved you, so you must love one another. By this all men will know that you are my disciples, if you love one another. (John 13:34–35)

> We love because he first loved us. If anyone says, "I love God," yet hates his brother, he is a liar. For anyone who does not love his brother, whom he has seen, cannot love God, whom he has not seen. And he has given us this command: Whoever loves God must also love his brother. (1 John 4:19–21)

Having a good relationship with God takes care of the selfish thinking called "self-esteem."

Many people wrestle with both kinds of selfish thinking (thinking too highly of themselves but also thinking it is right to feel like a nobody). It can feel natural to assume that when you are in bad shape it is the better, humbler position to think of yourself as a nobody.[1]

These two perspectives can exist either at the same time or back and forth. If they alternate, that does not show that you have gone from loving yourself to not loving yourself. It just shows that there are two different expressions of self-love. The way out is to keep your thoughts on God and on others.

> For by the grace given me I say to every one of you: Do not think of yourself more highly than you ought, but rather think of yourself with sober judgment, in accordance with the measure of faith God has given you. Just as each of us has one body with many members, and these members do not all have the same function, so in Christ we who are many form one body, and each member belongs to all the others. We have different gifts, according to the grace given us. If a man's gift is prophesying, let him use it in proportion to his faith. If it is serving, let him serve; if it is teaching, let him teach; if it is encouraging, let him encourage; if it is contributing to the needs of others, let him give generously; if it is leadership, let him govern diligently; if it is showing mercy, let him do it cheerfully. (Rom. 12:3–8)

---

1. Supposed humility is the same kind of view, and we *all* struggle with this one. We think we are better than other people, even in our humility.

Accept the gifts that God has given you, and use them. Do not assume that if you are using what God has given you, you are being an extrovert in a wrong kind of way. Using your gifts is normal. For instance, I believed I should be teaching, but there was a time in my life where if I got up in front of anyone, I would take glory for my ability to do it. Sometimes that still happens, but not like it used to. I have accepted that God has given me this gift, and I am to use it. It is right. It is what God gave it to you for.

If you have a talent and you say, "Using this would draw inordinate attention to myself. I will be humble and not use it," that is wrong. You can think of yourself as being spiritual while you are *not* using your gift and wind up listening to someone else who is using his gift and be critical of him. Do not be critical of him and of yourself and think that you are being spiritual by denying your gifts. Whatever He has given you, use it.

Chapter 4
HOW TO WALK IN THE LIGHT

> This is the message we have heard from him and declare to you: God is light; in him there is no darkness at all. (1 John 1:5)

EVEN IN A WELL-LIT ROOM, there are shadows. Outside it is brighter, but there is darkness out there, too. As I look out the window from my desk, I see an apple tree with six inches of snow on each branch. That tree is "white as snow," but even it is in darkness because the sky is overcast. David prayed in Psalm 51:7, "Cleanse me with hyssop, and I will be clean;

wash me, and I will be whiter than snow." God is light, and in Him there is *no darkness at all*.

"But if we walk in the light, as he is in the light, we have fellowship with one another, and the blood of Jesus, his Son, purifies us from all sin" (1 John 1:7). The word *purifies* means "keeps on cleansing." It is a continuous washing. Walking in the light means that as soon as you sin, you are aware of it, you confess it, and it gets cleansed. The result? We have fellowship with one another. Walking in the light does not mean never sinning, but it does mean that obedience is your normal state of being.

"We proclaim to you what we have seen and heard so that you also may have fellowship with us. And our fellowship is with the Father and with His Son Jesus Christ" (1 John 1:3). When we are walking in the light, we also have fellowship with God.

This booklet has given you instruction on how to be free from depression, false guilt, and low self-esteem. Now your goal is to stay free. That means staying cleansed from those sins, and in order to get that cleansing, you need to know when you have sinned. You are most likely to notice your sin when you are in the light.

> In the year that King Uzziah died, I saw the Lord seated on a throne, high and exalted, and the train of his robe filled the temple. Above him were seraphs, each with six wings: With two wings they covered their

faces, with two they covered their feet, and with two they were flying. And they were calling to one another:

> "Holy, holy, holy is the LORD Almighty;
> the whole earth is full of his glory."

At the sound of their voices the doorposts and thresholds shook and the temple was filled with smoke.

"Woe to me!" I cried. "I am ruined! For I am a man of unclean lips, and I live among a people of unclean lips, and my eyes have seen the King, the LORD Almighty."

Then one of the seraphs flew to me with a live coal in his hand, which he had taken with tongs from the altar. With it he touched my mouth and said, "See, this has touched your lips; your guilt is taken away and your sin atoned for." (Isa. 6:1–7)

In the presence of complete light, Isaiah saw his sinfulness, confessed, and was cleansed immediately.

How do you walk in the light? First, *confess every sin to God as soon as you are aware of it.* "If we confess our sins, he is faithful and just and will forgive us our sins and purify us from all unrighteousness" (1 John 1:9). God forgives the sins we confess to Him, and He forgives them right away. This cleanses us whiter than snow and gets us back into the light.

Often, we sin for a while, get clean, sin for a while, get clean, sin for a while . . . That is the method of the average Christian. That is not walking in the light! Walking in the light continually cleanses. When we make a habit of keeping short accounts with God, it becomes more natural to be obedient. When we disobey, we are brought up short right away, and the sin gets cleansed right away.

The Scripture says, "Light has come into the world, but men loved darkness instead of light because their deeds were evil. Everyone who does evil hates the light, and will not come into the light for fear that his deeds will be exposed. But whoever lives by the truth comes into the light, so that it may be seen plainly that what he has done has been done through God" (John 3:19–21). When you walk in the light, you are *asking* to be reproved. Some children do everything to hide what they have done wrong. Others do everything to get caught. They want to be corrected. God wants us to be the kind of people who *want* to get caught.

The trouble is that when you are in sin, you won't want to come to the light. The solution? Program yourself ahead of time for what you will do when you get into sin. Suppose I am in flight training, and there's a red handle in the cockpit marked *Eject*. I don't practice pulling the red handle. But I program my head so that if the wrong lights go on or there's smoke in the cockpit, I don't need to stop and debate with myself about what to do. I pull the red handle! I am trained to eject in certain situations.

When things are going well, program yourself to say, "Turn to the light; turn to the light; turn to the light." When something goes wrong, that training will tell you to turn back to God.

Another aspect of walking in the light is *spending time with the Lord every single day in the Word and in prayer*. We will look at prayer first.

Get into the habit of praying. I am not a very good "prayer" when it comes to setting aside time and praying for an hour straight. I am much better at praying all the time. If I'm walking, running, or sitting, if I'm driving, if I'm thinking, I talk to God.

Mostly I talk about people. I don't talk to God about myself much, unless I'm in trouble. Years ago, InterVarsity staff member Bill Steeper said, "It was a wonderful thing when I got myself off my own hands." He turned himself over to God.

Corrie ten Boom said the same thing to me. She was riding in the back of a car one night on a dangerous road. The driver was going way too fast, and she was terrified. She decided to spend the time interceding for other people. When she prayed for others, her fear disappeared.

And so it was, after the LORD had spoken these words to Job, that the LORD said to Eliphaz the Temanite, "My wrath is aroused against you and your two friends, for you have not spoken of Me what is right, as My servant Job has. Now therefore, take for yourselves seven bulls and seven rams, go to My servant Job, and offer up for yourselves a burnt offering; and My servant Job shall pray for you. For I will accept him, lest I deal with you according to your folly; because you have not spoken of Me what is right, as My servant Job has." So Eliphaz the Temanite and Bildad the Shuhite and Zophar the Naamathite went and did as the LORD commanded them; for the LORD had accepted Job. *And the Lord restored Job's losses when he prayed for his friends.* Indeed the LORD gave Job twice as much as he had before. (Job 42:7–10 NKJV)

Job had repented, and the Lord had accepted him, but it was when Job interceded for his friends that the Lord acted to restore his fortunes. Make it a habit to intercede for others every day. No family is without problems. My family has had our share of them. What has helped us most is not letting ourselves get wrapped up in the problems. When we keep interceding for and being concerned about others, we don't have time to be too concerned about ourselves.

One of the first times I spoke on this subject was after the birth and death of our little granddaughter Alexa. My daughter-in-law Meredith was two weeks overdue. Alexa was 9 lbs. 10 oz., the labor was long, and she was born not breathing. Two of the nurses were in tears. Meredith was comforting one nurse, and my son Gordon was comforting the other. That's the way it was for the next fifteen months until Alexa died. When you give yourself to other people, God gives you extra grace for your own troubles.

You need to make a choice. Choose to always turn up to God; don't ever turn inward. Turning inward is a downhill spiral.

> "Doubtless," said I, "what it utters is its only stock and store
> Caught from some unhappy master whom unmerciful Disaster
> Followed fast and followed faster till his songs one burden bore—
> Till the dirges of his Hope that melancholy burden bore
> Of 'Never—nevermore.'"[2]

Do not turn in! Turn up to the light and turn out to others.

When you look *up* instead of in, you will become aware of your sin, but once you are aware of it, it can be taken care of right away. You will be back in the joy of the Lord quickly. When you look out, you will be concerned about others, for their benefit.

2. Edgar Allan Poe, *"The Raven."*

Next, *spend time in the Word.* "The Bible will keep you from sin, or sin will keep you from the Bible."[3]

> The law of the LORD is perfect, converting the soul;
> The testimony of the LORD is sure, making wise the simple;
> The statutes of the LORD are right, rejoicing the heart;
> The commandment of the LORD is pure, enlightening the eyes;
> The fear of the LORD is clean, enduring forever;
> The judgments of the LORD are true and righteous altogether.
> More to be desired are they than gold,
> Yea, than much fine gold;
> Sweeter also than honey and the honeycomb.
> Moreover by them Your servant is warned,
> And in keeping them there is great reward.
> Who can understand his errors?
> Cleanse me from secret faults.
> Keep back Your servant also from presumptuous sins;
> Let them not have dominion over me.
> Then I shall be blameless,
> And I shall be innocent of great transgression.
> Let the words of my mouth and the meditation of my heart

---

3. Dwight L. Moody

Be acceptable in Your sight,
O LORD, my strength and my Redeemer.
(Psalm 19:7–14 NKJV)

The law of the Lord is perfect, and it converts the soul. God's revelation revives, awakens, and changes men. His Word makes us wise, it rejoices, it enlightens, it endures.

When you read the Word, do you have a sense that you are immersed in something that is perfect, right, sure, clean, and righteous altogether? Are you enraptured by it? The Psalmist was. "More to be desired are they than gold, yea, than much fine gold" (v. 10). He desired God's Word for wealth—perfect wealth, fine gold. "Sweeter also than honey and the honeycomb" (v. 10). He desired it for taste—a pleasure he genuinely enjoyed.

Do you desire the Word of God like you desire wealth? Do you desire it like you desire honey? Does it taste sweet to you? We should have a great desire for the Word of God.

There have been times in my life when I would read the Word, and it seemed rather dead—and other times when I just couldn't get enough of it in quantity or in quality. I would be so wrapped up in it that I wouldn't know whether to go on to the next passage or go back and repeat. I wanted more, and I also didn't want to lose what I'd just gotten, because it was so precious, so sweet, so wonderful. It really revives the soul, it really makes wise the simple, it really rejoices the heart, it really enlightens the eyes.

What else does God's revelation do? "Moreover by them Your servant is warned" (v. 11). It warns us. "And in keeping them there is great reward" (v. 11). When we obey these testimonies from God, there is great reward.

"Who can understand his errors? Cleanse me from secret faults" (v. 12). For most of my life, I assumed that "secret faults" were sins that I wasn't aware of, and that we are to use this as a prayer of general confession after we have confessed the sins we know. Then I was spending time in *The Treasury of David* (Spurgeon's commentary on the Psalms), and I found that very few people thought that. They said it meant, "Keep me from hiding my sins," the way David tried to hide his. Of course, there is no sense in trying to hide the sins we do openly—everyone knows about them already. Certain sins we do privately: things we think, things we say. Those are harder to confess—just the fact that we hid them in the first place means we don't want to acknowledge them, because that would require bringing them out into the open before God. The psalmist asks God to expose the things he is hiding. That had happened to him. When David thought he had hidden his sin of adultery and murder, it took the prophet Nathan to tell him a parable and bring it out into the open.

Hiding sin is deadly. We might think nobody knows about it, and nobody's going to know. We end up deceiving ourselves. There was a poem written in the 1800s about a man who murdered someone and buried him in a deep, dark stream. He went back the next day and found that the stream bed had gone dry, and there lay the corpse out in the open. He covered the corpse with leaves, and the wind blew them away. He realized that even if he buried the body ten thousand fathoms deep, he wasn't going to get away with the murder.

> Down went the corse with hollow plunge
>   And vanish'd in the pool;
> Anon I cleans'd my bloody hands,
>   And wash'd my forehead cool,
> And sat among the urchins young,
>   That evening in the school.
> . . . .
>
> Heavily I rose up, as soon
>   As light was in the sky,
> And sought the black accursed pool
>   With a wild misgiving eye:
> And I saw the Dead in the river bed,
>   For the faithless stream was dry.
> . . . .
>
> With breathless speed, like a soul in chase,
>   I took him up and ran;
> There was no time to dig a grave
>   Before the day began:

> In a lonesome wood, with heaps of leaves,
>   I hid the murder'd man.
>
> And all that day I read in school,
>   But my thought was other where;
> As soon as the mid-day task was done,
>   In secret I was there;
> And a mighty wind had swept the leaves,
>   And still the corse was bare!
>
> Then down I cast me on my face,
>   And first began to weep,
> For I knew my secret then was one
>   That earth refus'd to keep:
> Or land or sea, though he should be
>   Ten thousand fathoms deep.
>
> So wills the fierce avenging Sprite,
>   Till blood for blood atones!
> Aye, though he's buried in a cave,
>   And trodden down with stones,
> And years have rotted off his flesh,—
>   The world shall see his bones.[4]

Lord, cleanse Thou me from the things I am hiding.

---

4. Thomas Hood, "The Dream of Eugene Aram."

"Who can understand his errors?" (v. 12). We may not understand our own sin because of our remarkable ability to self-deceive. The Word of God reveals our errors.

"Keep back Your servant also from presumptuous sins" (v. 13). A presumptuous sin is something that you have *not* deceived yourself about. You knew it was wrong, but you had the audacity to do it anyway. By man's valuation, it may not be a very big sin, but it is deliberate—for instance, a white lie. We dare to lie, and God tells us that He has prepared a lake of fire for all liars. We dare to lie, and the Word says God hates liars. We don't hide presumptuous sins; we pull them off because everyone else is doing them, too. David asks God to keep him away from such sin.

"Let them not have dominion over me" (v. 13). I do it, I know it is wrong, and I do it again, and again, and again. Pretty soon, this sin has me in a vise. It has power over me, and I cannot keep from doing it. It may be an "acceptable" sin because everyone else is presuming it, too. But unless I am kept back from it, I end up as its slave. Let them not have dominion over me.

"Then I shall be blameless, and I shall be innocent of great transgression" (v. 13). I counsel many people who have committed great transgressions. They confess the sin, and God forgives them—and they turn right around and do it again. They confess it again, and they do it again. One man came to me for help with this. He would commit the sin, confess it, be forgiven, and immediately he would be right back in temptation. He would fall over the cliff again, confess, and find himself tottering on the edge once more. He asked me, "Why do I keep doing this when I have confessed it each time?"

If he would take care of his other sins, he would be far away from the edge. The reason people keep doing big sins over and over is that they have not been delivered from the presumptuous sins and the secret sins that led up to them. The man who keeps falling is confessing his great sins, but he isn't confessing his little ones.

When people file for divorce, generally the situation is so bad, and they hate each other so much, that it seems like there is no way to correct it. They did not anticipate this when they got married. If they had been kept from secret sins and presumptuous sins, the divorce would never have happened.

The way to stay away from big sins is to stay away from little ones. Don't put up with *any* sin in yourself. Keep your little sins confessed so that they cannot get dominion over you. I don't have to worry about ever committing a great transgression if I am kept from minor ones. If I am constantly confessing the secret sins and the presumptuous sins, the devil can't get close to me on a big one. He won't even try.

People have often asked me why I never have any big sin problems and why my family isn't messed up like many other families. Simple. We take care of the secret sins and the presumptuous ones. It's not that we're favored. We aren't. The devil simply knows that he can't trip us up with great temptations, so he works on us with little ones (or he keeps trying to, anyway). He knows he cannot get us into the eighth grade in sin until we pass the first grade. As long as I keep flunking the devil's first grade, I get held back, and I don't make it to his advanced courses. Make sure you are flunking the devil's first grade.

"Let the words of my mouth and the meditation of my heart be acceptable in Thy sight, O LORD, my Rock and my Redeemer" (v. 14). Many people, even Christians, don't particularly care what they say in public or to whom they say it. Some of us care very much. We think that if we pass the public approval on what we say, we're OK.

David wasn't satisfied with that. He said, "Let the words of my mouth and the meditation of my heart be acceptable in *Your* sight, O God." When we ask the Lord to make what we think about in our hearts and say with our mouths acceptable in *His* sight, not just in other people's sight, we don't have to worry about any great transgression.

We can pass this to our children as well. We are used to laying out rules for them to make their actions acceptable in our sight. Suppose we could teach our children so that the meditation of their hearts would be acceptable in the sight of God? If our children were like that, how many rules would we have to lay down? Not many. Not many at all.

Here is how you can teach your children to meditate on the Lord and have their meditation be acceptable in His sight. First, keep *your* meditation acceptable in God's sight and the words of *your* mouth acceptable in His sight. How do you speak to your children? Is that how you speak to everyone else? The Scripture says, "Out of the abundance of the heart the mouth speaks" (Matt. 12:34 NKJV). When I take care of the meditation of my heart, I have already taken care of what I'm going to say. What you say is the result of what you're meditating on. If you are not meditating rightly, what you say will not be right either in content or in manner. Your children will pick it up and meditate right back to you that way.

James 3 says that out of the same mouth proceed blessing and cursing, and that should not be. Ask God to make the meditation of your heart acceptable in His sight. That is the solution for holy, godly contact. That is where to start. Start with *your* heart, *your* motivation. Then you can go on to your children's hearts, your children's motivations.

Go back to dealing with secret sins. Go back to presumptuous sins. Go back to the words of your mouth and the meditations of your heart. When you get those things acceptable in God's sight, you won't have to worry about falling over any cliffs.

It is easy to fixate on big sins and let anything less than them pass for OK. You are doing something little that is not right, and someone says, "What's wrong with that?" That's what wrong with it—*saying*, "What's wrong with it?" What's wrong is wanting to say that anything less than a big sin is OK.

We live as if sin were the same as crime. If it's not violating the law, then it's alright. If it's not *literally* violating the Ten Commandments, it's OK. But Jesus said that "anyone who looks at a woman lustfully has already committed adultery with her in his heart" (Matt. 5:28). God is after the meditation of your heart. The person who solves the problem there doesn't have to worry about the act of adultery. The person who solves the problem of hatred never has to worry about murder. The person who solves the problem of coveting never has to worry about stealing. Go after the basic things. Go after the heart sins underneath.

What if you are already guilty of the basic things? God forgives those like He forgives great transgressions. But you have to admit it first. You have to call it sin. You may have a good reputation with your friends and family, but you are miserable in your heart. If so, start asking God to search your heart.

Recently I reread a letter I received in the 1970s from the wife of a Navy captain of the Naval Academy Class of '53. Her husband had just told her that that as soon as the seniors of the class of 1950 graduated at the end of his plebe year, the plebes (the freshmen) went through all the seniors' rooms to see if they had left anything behind.

This man was not a Christian. He was searching through the dorms, and he came to my room. He pulled open the locker door, and on the inside panel was pasted Psalm 139:9: "If I take the wings of the morning, and dwell in the uttermost parts of the sea, even there Thy hand shall lead me, and Thy right hand shall hold me." That struck him. He became a Christian shortly thereafter, and twenty-six years later, I found out that that verse of Scripture pasted up in my locker door had helped bring him to the Lord.

Psalm 139 is the greatest cure there is for secret sins. It is the story of a man trying to run away from God and not succeeding. Verse 23 says, "Search me, O God, and know my heart. Try me and know my thoughts, and see if there be any wicked way in me, and lead me in the way everlasting." If you don't know what the problem is, ask God to search you. Then in prevention of future sin, ask Him to cause the meditation of your heart to be acceptable in His sight.

Look back at Psalm 19. David's great desire and delight came from the Word of God. The Word of God is light; the Word of God is a joy. If you do not know how to meditate in an acceptable way, dwell in the Scriptures, and you will come to find them like gold, like much fine gold. Your heart will change directly proportional to how much time you spend in the Word of God.

The last aspect of walking in the light that I will mention here is *being thankful*. This will help with *many* areas of your life. Start by recognizing that God is the Creator of all things. Look at all the trees, all the flowers, all the clouds, stars, sun, and moon. Thank God. Then thank God for all of your family. Thank Him for everything you have. Thank Him out loud, and be specific.

> Give thanks in all circumstances; for this is God's will for you in Christ Jesus. (1 Thess. 5:18)

> Do not be anxious about anything, but in everything, by prayer and petition, with thanksgiving, present your requests to God. And the peace of God, which transcends all understanding, will guard your hearts and your minds in Christ Jesus. (Phil. 4:6–7)

Giving thanks is God's will for you. It results in peace that passes all comprehension.

> I have not stopped giving thanks for you, remembering you in my prayers. (Eph. 1:16)

> I thank my God every time I remember you. In all my prayers for all of you, I always pray with joy because of your partnership in the gospel from the first day until now, being confident of this, that he who began a good work in you will carry it on to completion until the day of Christ Jesus. (Phil. 1:3–6)

Being thankful is an exercise of the will in obeying God's command to be thankful in everything. I did not want to be sick this week, but I can be thankful in this circumstance of being sick. When I am thankful in everything, then I can rejoice always. When I make my petitions to God with thankfulness, I end up with peace.

One of the signs of walking in the light is *singing*. This is not a way to walk in the light, but a result of it. When you walk in the light, you may end up singing to the Lord, even if you don't know any great hymns.

I knew one young woman who had been "converted" several times and still wasn't saved. She had read every book in the Christian bookstore and gone to every counselor in town. She went to multiple people for counseling, attended our school of practical Christianity, and read several books. I met with her and her husband a couple times and with her more times. She knew all the answers but did not seem able to put them into effect in her life.

One day she showed up at our front door. Bessie met her and told her to go sit in one of the chairs under the apple tree in the backyard while she went to find me.

At that moment, I was reading a book by Watchman Nee, and I had just read a paragraph where Nee said (to paraphrase), "Two men can hear the same text preached at the same time. 'I am the way the truth and the life; no man cometh to the Father but by me.' One person will hear that text and say, 'Oh, that's wonderful!' and will come to the Father through Jesus Christ. Another person will say, 'Oh, what a wonderful doctrine!' and come to the doctrine."

Having just read that paragraph, I quoted it to the young woman under the apple tree. She asked me, "What is the difference between the two?"

I said, "The first has love, joy, and peace, and the other has a plaque on the wall."

The next day she called to tell me that she was not a Christian. I replied that I did not think she was, either. She got upset with me because I agreed with her.

I told her that I would not tell her how to become a Christian. Her head was filled with the gospel already. If I told her, she would go through the motions and not be any more saved afterward. I said, "I'm not going to tell you how to become a Christian, because you are a doer, and you'd just go plug the formula. You've plugged it several times already, and nothing's happened. If I tell you how to come to the Father, you won't understand it. Grace, love, faith: all these terms you know by heart are empty words to you. There are certain things you need to find out for yourself first. You have to find out that God is holy. You have to find out how awfully sinful you are. You have to find out how great the love of God is. After you have some glimmer of the holiness of God, and after you have some small understanding of how sinful you are in the light of that holiness, and after you begin to see how much love God has for you in your sinfulness, then I will tell you the good news."

I did not hear from her for several weeks. Then she called and asked, "How could the Father love the Son and send Him to the cross?" She was starting to understand.

"Oh!" I replied. "It didn't say He loved the Son. It says, 'For God so loved the *world* that He gave His only begotten Son.' That tells us not how much He loves the Son, but how much He loves the world."

I realized that she probably had enough understanding for me to tell her the gospel. However, I wanted to speak to her heart. Her head was already filled with truth, but it had not sunk in. I decided to give her the gospel in song and poetry. Over the phone, I sang her hymns like *The Love of God, The Deep, Deep Love of Jesus*, and *At Calvary*.

Sometime later, she was working a job cleaning apartments. As she ran the vacuum, she was singing, "He is Lord, He is Lord, He has risen from the dead, and He is Lord," and she was saved in the middle of the chorus. She was looking up to God, and her conversion was real.

Walking in the light is a grace and faith event. There is no other way. Colossians 2:6 (ESV) says, "Therefore, as you received Christ Jesus the Lord, so walk in Him." How did you receive Christ Jesus the Lord? By effort? By trying? No. You quit trying when you received Christ Jesus the Lord, and you trusted. When you quit trying and trusted grace, the Lord changed your life.

"Therefore, as you received Christ Jesus the Lord, so walk in Him." The same procedure by which I was saved is the way I live the Christian life. When I became a Christian, I quit trying—and having become one, I still quit trying. Living the Christian life is like being born again every instant. It's grace and faith. You didn't try to get in, and you don't try to live.

You say, "Yes, I do."

Well, tell me this: do you succeed?

People come to me and say, "Jim, I don't know why I failed. I *tried* to live the Christian life."

"Oh," I say, "that's why. You fell because you tried to live the Christian life."

We are not to try to live the Christian life. Walking in the light is grace, faith, grace, faith. As soon as we get saved, we are tempted to revert to trying. We are not to do that. The entire book of Galatians was written against that. Paul said, "Oh foolish Galatians!" (Gal. 3:1). You idiots! Tell me how you got into this kingdom. "Did you receive the Spirit by the works of the law, or by the hearing of faith? Are you so foolish? Having been made alive by the Spirit, are you now made perfect by the flesh?" (Gal. 3:2–3).

Look up to God and reject trying. This is what the New Testament teaches. We read it and hear something else. We try to reinterpret everything into something we can do. Do not read this Scripture and go back to trying.

"If I don't try, I'll fall."

If you do try, you'll fall.

A multitude of groups today are out there teaching the secret way to the "deeper life," and seekers flock to them by the thousands. Those ways don't work. This is true, and it works, but people aren't flocking to it—because they don't want to walk in the light. They want a quick fix that doesn't require so much cleaning of their hearts. They would rather try, or they would rather have a periodic cleansing.

Christians today do not walk in complete joy, nor are they whiter than snow. They are living subnormal Christian lives. However, it is possible to walk in the light as He is in the light. That way, you do not have to get rid of the sins discussed in the previous chapters, because you will not fall into them.

I used to be a "tryer" and a charger, and the Lord spared me. I am "doing" more with less effort now than I used to do with effort. This is so contrary to our normal mode of thinking that it may not make sense to you. Ask God to help it make sense so that you can reject trying and trust Him.[5] Books that have helped me walk in the light and live by faith instead of by trying include *The Calvary Road*, *We Would See Jesus*, and *Broken People, Transforming Grace: The Gospel's Message of Saving Love* by Roy Hession and *Continuous Revival* by Norman Grubb.

5. For more on living by grace through faith, read my book *Dead and Alive: Obedience and the New Man*, available at Amazon.com and ccmbooks.org.

www.ingramcontent.com/pod-product-compliance
Lightning Source LLC
Chambersburg PA
CBHW052207110526
44591CB00012B/2115